YOUR KNOWLEDGE HAS VALUE

AF153437

- We will publish your bachelor's and
  master's thesis, essays and papers

- Your own eBook and book -
  sold worldwide in all relevant shops

- Earn money with each sale

Upload your text at www.GRIN.com
and publish for free

Blasted Masculinity. An Analysis of Manhood and Male Conflicts in Sarah Kane's "Blasted"

Timmy Paul

Bibliographic information published by the German National Library:

The German National Library lists this publication in the National Bibliography; detailed bibliographic data are available on the Internet at http://dnb.dnb.de.

ISBN: 9783346579713
This book is also available as an ebook.

© GRIN Publishing GmbH
Nymphenburger Straße 86
80636 München

Print and binding: Books on Demand GmbH, Norderstedt, Germany
Printed on acid-free paper from responsible sources.

The present work has been carefully prepared. Nevertheless, authors and publishers do not incur liability for the correctness of information, notes, links and advice as well as any printing errors.

GRIN web shop: https://www.grin.com/document/1169242

Technische Universität Carolo-Wilhelmina zu Braunschweig

Institut für Anglistik und Amerikanistik

Modul M2

Dystopian Theatre

Wintersemester 2019/2020

Hausarbeit

Blasted Masculinity

An Analysis of Manhood and Male Conflicts in Sarah Kane's *Blasted*

Name: Timmy Paul

Studiengang: Master of Education, English Studies und Geschichte

Fachsemester: 5.

Inhaltsverzeichnis

1. Introduction...3

2. What is Masculinity?..4

    2.1 Definition of Masculinity...4

    2.2 The Concept of Hegemonic Masculinity...6

3. Masculinity in Sarah Kane's Blasted..8

    3.1 Ian and Cate...8

    3.2 The Soldier and Ian...13

4. Conclusion 16

Works cited..18

1. Introduction

"You never fucked a man before you killed him?" (Kane 3.47) This quote can be seen as the foretaste of what happens next in Sarah Kane's notorious play *Blasted*. At the time of its release, the play provoked a major public outcry because of its presentation of raw violence and breathtaking cruelty. (Iball 1) Critics heavily attacked then 23-years old playwright Sarah Kane and called her play a "disgusting feast of filth" (Benedict). Sarah Kane herself did not understand the criticism and claimed: "I'm simply trying to tell the truth about human behaviour as I see it." (Benedict) She continues: "Take the glamour out of violence and it becomes utterly repulsive. Would people seriously prefer it if the violence was appealing?" (Benedict). Irrespective of what her critics said about her work, the play became one of the most famous representatives of the so called 'In-Yer-Face-Theatre'. (Iball 12)

The characters of the play are two men and a woman. The plot begins in an expensive hotel room in Leeds, as Ian, a journalist who appears to be racist and abusive and Cate, his simple-minded, but good natured ex-girlfriend enter the stage. During the first two scenes, it is shown that Ian abuses Cate mentally and physically. He eventually rapes her off-stage. The scenes are clearly dominated by his male violence against her. The setting soon turns into an apocalyptic scenery, since Kane wanted to add an impression of the Bosnian War. (Saunders 38-39) As soon as the third character, the soldier, enters the stage, the violence reaches its peak. Ian, who was dominant and abusive until then, gets abused himself by the soldier, a truly cold-blooded, not to say purely evil man and hence is turned into an obedient and pitiable person, hardly with any bit of masculinity left. The quote from the beginning of this paper is the initiation of a process, that culminates in the destruction of Ian's masculinity.

In this paper, I would like to investigate this phenomenon. In order to do so, I will examine R. W. Connell's concept of hegemonic masculinity and compare it to the male characters in Sarah Kane's *Blasted*. My research questions for this term paper are: What exactly is hegemonic masculinity? What are the characteristics of Ian's and the soldier's masculinities? What is the relationship between them? How is the representation of masculinity connected to the play's overall message?

In the following chapters, I will examine the concept of masculinity, especially the concept of hegemonic masculinity, that was first mentioned by Raewyn Connell, in her book *Masculinities*. Then, I will analyse the different types of masculinity that are displayed by the characters in Sarah Kane's *Blasted*. Eventually, I will finish this paper by concluding the overall outcome, answering the research questions and providing a suggestion for further research.

2. What is Masculinity?

2.1 Definition of Masculinity

In her book *Masculinities*, Raewyn Connell plausibly argues that the term 'masculinity' can hardly be defined. Different philosophical systems came up with attempts to define what maleness is but none of them were able to do it in an entirely satisfying way.

However, Connell explains that the term 'masculinity' is based on the conception of individuality that came up in early-modernist Europe. She calls 'masculinity' a construct, that cannot exist without its counterpart 'femininity'. (Connell 68) According to her, "A culture which does not treat women and men as bearers of polarized character types, at least in principle, does not have a concept of masculinity in the sense of modern European/American culture." (Connell 68) Prior to that, women have been seen rather as "[...] incomplete or inferior examples of the same character (for instance, having less of the faculty of reason)." (68) Connell states, that this concept emerged together with "[...] the bourgeois ideology of 'separate spheres' in the nineteenth century" (68) and, considering this, the concept of masculinity is no more than a few hundred years old. (Connell 68) Furthermore, she claims that there is nothing such as an universal truth or universal knowledge about masculinity, since gender is culturally different constructed in every society or culture. (Connell 68)

According to Connell, there have been four different strategies to define 'masculinity'. First of all, Essentialists tried to explain men's lives based on a specific supposedly masculine feature, like risk-taking, being aggressive or being more responsible or irresponsible. (Connell 68-69)

4

Positivists tried to produce "facts" about what masculinity is and claimed that masculinity is "[...] what men actually are." (Connell 69) Connell argues that these are problematic, since their descriptions are themselves based on assumptions about gender. She mentions that there already occurs a differentiation between "men" and "women" when one seeks to measure what men do and what women do. This is, as Connel mentions, "[...] unavoidably a process of social attribution using common-sense typologies of gender." (69) Also, this approach blinds out the fact as well that there are women, who act masculine and men, who act feminine. (Connell 69)

Moreover, she describes the normative definition of masculinity, that implies, that masculinity is, how men ought to be. Again, this is a rather problematic approach, since most of the men do not match these 'norms'. (Connell 70)

Finally, the semiotic approach, which is based on the "[...] formulae of structural linguistics, where elements of speech are defined by their differences from each other" (Connell 70) describes masculinity as a system of symbolic differences between male and female characteristics. The definition concludes that masculinity is, what is not femininity. (Connell 70)

In contrast to this, Connell argues that masculinity rather must be seen as "[...] simultaneously a place in gender relations, the practices through which men and women engage that place in gender, and the effects of these practices in bodily experience, personality and culture." (Connell 71) Concerning the purpose of the term 'masculinity', she claims that "The terms 'masculine' and 'feminine' point beyond categorical sex difference to the ways men differ among themselves, and women differ among themselves, in matters of gender." (Connell 69)

In order to understand what 'masculinity' is in relationship to its counterpart 'femininity', Connell explains that "Gender is a way in which social practice is ordered." (Connell 71) She claims that everyone's daily life is "[...] organized in relation to a reproductive area [...]" (Connell 71), which includes "[...] sexual arousal and intercourse, childbirth and infant care, bodily sex difference and similarity." (71) As a third configuration of gender, Connell names institutions as substantively structured by gender. (Connell 73) To serve as an example, she identifies the state to be a masculine institution, having a connection between the organization of practice and the reproductive arena. (Connell

73) Connell states that most of the representatives of the state are men and that "[...] there is a gender configuring of recruitment and promotion, a gender configuring of the internal division of labour and systems of control, a gender configuring of policymaking, practical routines, and ways of mobilizing pleasure and consent." (Connell 73)

Furthermore, there is an interaction between gender and other social structures, like race and class. As an example, the social structure of white men's masculinity is not only constructed in relation to white femininity, but to different kinds of masculinity, like black masculinity, as well. (Connell 75) Considering the fact that there is not only one white masculinity or one black masculinity, it becomes clear, that there is a large number of masculinities, but femininities as well, that are different amongst each other.

2.2 The Concept of Hegemonic Masculinity

Now that we have considered, that instead of just one masculinity or just one white or black masculinity, there is a large scale of masculinities, taking into consideration race, class and gender, which have developed and since then exist in relation to each other, we need to analyse the gender relations between them. Connell describes, that there is one specific masculinity that occupies the position of hegemony and which is "[...] always contestable." (Connell 76) She describes that at any time one specific form of masculinity is in charge of the "[...] leading position in social life." (77) She calls it "[...] the configuration of gender practice which embodies the currently accepted answer to the problem of the legitimacy of patriarchy, which guarantees (or is taken to guarantee) the dominant position of men and the subordination of women." (77) Thus, Connell explains the task of hegemonic masculinity as maintaining the patriarchy, by ensuring the male dominion and the female subordination. (Connell 77)

Furthermore, she argues that there must be a correspondence between the cultural ideal and institutionalized power, like the government, the military or business in order to establish the hegemony. (Connell 77) She emphasizes that 'hegemonic masculinity' is a strategy in order to establish patriarchy, hence if the need for an alternative strategy for defending patriarchy occurs, the position of hegemony may be occupied by a new kind of masculinity. (Connell 77)

6

According to her, 'hegemonic masculinity' is the construction of the dominance of one group and the subordination of other groups. To give an example, in the Western European/American society, heterosexual men are the dominant group, whereas homosexual men are the subordinate one. (Connell 78) The subordination is obviously not voluntary but rather forced by oppression and discrimination. (Connell 78) Connell states, that this happens by "[...] political and cultural exclusion, cultural abuse [...], legal violence [...], street violence [...], economic discrimination and personal boycotts." (78) In doing so, homosexual masculinity is put to the bottom of hierarchy in men's gender relations. Homosexuality has become a symbol for everything, that has been banned from the self-concept of hegemonic masculinity and thereby locating it next to femininity. (Connell 78-79)

But also heterosexuals, who do not fit into the concept of 'hegemonic masculinity' are being excluded by being symbolically connected to femininity. To give an example, Connell recites terms like "[...] wimp, milksop, nerd, turkey, sissy, lily liver, jellyfish, yellowbelly, candy ass, ladyfinger, pushover, cookie pusher, cream puff, motherfucker, pantywaist, mother's boy, four-eye, ear-'ole, dweeb, geek, Milquetoast, Cedric, and so on." (Connell 79) All of these terms, are somehow at least symbolically related to femininity. (Connell 79)

And since, 'hegemonic masculinity' is described by Connell as not only heterosexual, but also white and privileged masculinity, it is obvious that there must be conflicts including race and class. Connell explains, that these conflicts can be seen in the USA, where on the one hand, male black sports stars for example can function as symbols of 'hegemonic masculinity', but on the other hand black males are depicted as brutish criminals by whites. (Connell 80) Furthermore, she claims that there is an interplay between race and class, since black unemployment and poverty can be traced back to institutionalized racism and discrimination, reminding us of the fact that the top positions of state, military and business are occupied by white males and thus of representatives of the 'hegemonic masculinity', who claim full authority. (Connel 80-81) She calls the relationship between masculinities of dominant and subordinate classes or ethnic groups 'marginalization'. (Connell 80) That means that for example male black celebrities might seen as examples for hegemonic masculinity, but their achievements like their fame

7

or their wealth do not have any effect on the authority of black men in general, implying that in the end they are more or less used as instruments by 'hegemonic masculinity'. (Connell 80-81)

This conception of 'hegemonic masculinity' has been criticized a number of times, as well. According to Demetrakis Z. Demetriou, Connell's concept of hegemonic masculinity, on the one hand "[...] represents the most influential and popular part [...]" (Demetriou 337) of her work, but on the other hand he criticizes that there apparently has not been any attempt "[...] to evaluate its theoretical merit." (337) Considering the critique of her concept, it has been reviewed and reshaped in 2005 by Connell and James W. Messerschmidt. In the article, the authors conclude that the key ideas, "[...] the combination of the plurality of masculinities and the hierarchy of masculinities" (Connell and Messerschmidt 846) remain the basis of the concept and other aspects like the "[...] too-simple model of the social relations surrounding hegemonic masculinities" (846-847) have to be discarded.

3. Masculinity in Sarah Kane's *Blasted*

3.1 Ian and Cate

After having a look at Connell's description of masculinity and hegemonic masculinity, how is this linked to Sarah Kane's *Blasted*? Actually, the audience can identify numerous examples of hegemonic masculinity within the play.

The plot begins with Ian and Cate entering an expensive hotel room in Leeds. In contrast to Ian, Kate Ashfield, who played Cate in the first performance of *Blasted*, calls Cate a simultaneously weak and strong character, because on the one hand she can't let go of Ian and on the other hand she fights back in various situations. (Saunders 164). It becomes quite clear, that both characters are supposed to represent the complete opposite of each other. As Connell mentioned in her book, in our western culture, the definition of 'masculinity', does not exist without the concept of 'femininity' as it's opposite. From the start, Ian exposes stereotypical "masculine" attributes. For example, while Cate "[...] stops at the door amazed at the classiness of the room" (Kane 1.3), examining

8

it and smelling the bouquet of flowers, Ian comments on the hotel room by simply saying "I've shat in better places than this." (1.3)

He excessively makes use of swearwords and bad language, offending not only people with migrational background but also Cate and her brother, who is a mentioned-only character. He claims that the city is being taken over by "wogs" and "pakis" (Kane 1.4), asks Cate if she is a "nigger-lover" and if she likes "[...] our coloured brethren" (1.5). He calls her brother a "retard" (1.5), a "spaz" (1.5) and a "joey" (1.5) because he is friends with some people of Indian descent. (1.5) As Cate mentions that they are "[...] really polite", Ian responds by saying "So they should be" (1.5), as if they should be glad to be allowed to live in Great Britain.

Ian's racism can be seen as a reference to "the man", which is a term defined by the Afro-American civil rights movement. As mentioned earlier, a white man's masculinity is not only constructed in relation to white women, but also to other men, in this case coloured men. (Connell 75) The term "the man" expresses coloured people's fear of white men's power over the police, courts and prisons in western countries, which derived from colonial times. The theory claims that white men make use of these institutions to oppress coloured men. (Connell 75) To give an example, Connell claims that in the US more coloured people end up in prison than whites. (Connell 75) Ian's sense of white supremacy and his view of people with a migrational background as parasites and as being not any more than guests in Western European societies displays strong parallels to the concept of "the man" and the idea of hegemonic masculinity.

Ian is shown to not only dislike coloured people, but also homosexuals, both men and women. While talking with Cate about his ex-wife Stella, he reveals that she left him for a woman. (Kane 1.18-1.19) He implies that Cate could be a lesbian, too, by stating she has got the potential for "sucking gash" (Kane 1.19) due to her clothing style. When asked if he ever had sex with a man, Ian becomes very defensive, pointing at his groin and claiming he does not "[...] dress like a cocksucker". (Kane 1.19) He then starts to rant about homosexuals, but also about coloured people and football fans by saying: "Hitler was wrong about the Jews who have they hurt the queers he should have gone for scum them and the wogs and fucking football fans send a bomber over Elland Road finish them off." (1.19) At this point, as a white, heterosexual male, who hates all the

9

other races and sexual orientations, Ian can be seen to perfectly fit into the depiction of hegemonic masculinity.

Another point worth to mention is, that Ian is shown to be fatally ill. In addition, he mentions a number of times that he stinks and therefore needs to take a shower, which, according to Saunders, symbolically implies that he, in contrast to Cate, is morally corrupted. (Saunders 43) This could be seen as a metaphor relating to their very different natures, since Ian is an abusive macho, whereas Cate seems to be caring and more or less innocent.

Considering Connell's concept, Ian can easily be identified as typical representative of the hegemonic masculinity. He ridicules and belittles everything, that he think to be "womanish", not "womanish" enough or unmanly. Besides the discrimination of homosexuals, there are other things he comments on negatively and tries to enforce his position. For example, when the room service brings them sandwiches, he makes fun of Cate, because she refuses to eat meat due to the fact that she is a vegetarian and is even disgusted by meat. (Kane 1.7) He also states that she looks "[...] like a lesbos" (Kane 1.7) because he finds her clothing not attractive and thereby inappropriate for a woman. As we can see, he discriminates, whatever is not part of his ideology which perfectly resembles hegemonic masculinity.

Another important factor in the play are guns. As Ian undresses in order to take a shower in the first scene, it is revealed that he brought a revolver with him. (Kane 1.3) It seems to be a source of power to him. During the first two scenes, Ian is seen to check his gun, constantly unloading and reloading it, taking it with him, when answering the door. (Kane 1.3, 1.4, 1.6, 1.8, 1.16, 2.26, 2.27) His thoughts seem to revolve around his gun, since he claims that he needs it to defend himself and Cate from people like him. (Kane 2.29) Although he claims that he won't hurt Cate, he puts the gun to her head after she falls unconscious, points it at her after she awakens (Kane 2.27) and threatens to shoot her. (Kane 2.31, 2.34) Furthermore, when Cate mentions that the new girlfriend of his ex-wife might be a nice person, he replies that she "[...] don't carry a gun". (Kane 1.18)

Connell explains that the gun can be seen as a symbol for the male genitalia. As an example, she mentions the NRA, who are, according to her, the defenders of hegemonic masculinity in the US and equal the loss of guns to the loss of masculinity. (Masculinities, 212) In scene 2, after being raped by Ian, Cate decides to stay in the hotel room in order to hurt him. When he comes back from the bathroom, she assaults him, beating, biting and kicking him and eventually manages to acquire the gun. She then points it at his groin, threatening to shoot. With his gun and subsequently his power taken away, he becomes submissive, desperately trying to comfort her in order to get the gun and thereby his power and masculinity back. (Kane 2.26)

Talking about the rape of Cate, it can be said that especially in the first scene, Ian seems to claim the right to have sex with her. In the beginning, when they talk about each others clothing, he undresses in front of her, ordering her to perform oral sex on him by saying the words "put your mouth on me". (Kane 1.7) Obviously, he takes it for granted that they are going to have sex. She responds by bursting out laughing, leaving him embarrassed. (Kane 1.8) By laughing at his genitalia, she laughs at his masculinity as well.

After a while, he makes another attempt kissing and touching her, but she panics and he has to comfort her. (Kane 1.14) He then blames her for turning him on and leaving him hanging, although in fact she did not reply to his advances. (Kane 1.14-1.15) He complains to her by saying things like "That wasn't really fair" (Kane 1.14) and "Leaving me hanging, making a prick of myself." (Kane 1.15) He eventually becomes angry and says "Don't pity me, Cate. You don't have to fuck me 'cause I'm dying, but don't push your cunt in my face then take it away 'cause I stick my tongue out." (Kane 1.15)

He humiliates her by imitating her stuttering and even gets her to apologize for her unwillingness to have sex with him. (Kane 1.15) Afterwards, he puts her hand on his genitals and starts masturbating with it, using her hand like an instrument, justifying it by claiming that he is in pain, since she turned him on and rejected to have sex with him. (Kane 1.15) This proves another time his notion of having a right to sleep with Cate.

Right after comforting her, and telling her that she does not have to worry about her "mistake", he asks her if they can have sex the night. (Kane 1.15) She rejects another time by stating that she promised to be Shaun's girlfriend, who is another mentioned-only character and apparently Cate's current boyfriend. (Kane 1.16) Ian does not accept this and claims that, since she did not have sex with Shaun but with him, when they were a couple, she is more his than Shaun's. (Kane 1.16) The way Ian talks about it, reveals that he claims Cate like an object or like a trophy and tries to outdo Shaun as a rival. He does not respect their relationship but rather sees it like a competition and tries to make clear that he owns her.

In the end of the first scene, Ian tries one last time to convince her to have sex with her. He claims to love her and says that she could make him happy. When she asks, how she should be able to do this, he responds by saying "You know" (Kane 1.23) suggesting sexual intercourse, which she denies another time, emphasizing that she does not love him. (Kane 1.23-1.24) Saunders adds, that in order to visualize how meaningless Ian's exclamation of love is, the bouquet of flowers he picks up and offers to Cate, are in the beginning of the next scene ripped apart and laying on the floor. (Saunders 41-42)

During the course of the scene, we learn that Ian has raped Cate during the night. The rape happened between the two scenes and very few detail about what happened exactly is revealed during the course of the second scene. In fact, it must have been very brutal, since she says "I can't piss. It's just blood [...] Or shit. It hurts." (Kane 2.34) and "You bit me. It's still bleeding." (Kane 2.32) She emphasizes multiple times, that she did not want to sleep with Ian throughout the scene, but Ian claims that she wanted to have sex with him. (Kane 2.31-2.32)

Connell states, that physical violence is part of hegemonic masculinity. As an example, she mentions how homosexual men are assaulted by heterosexual men, because some heterosexuals believe that they must punish homosexuals for "stepping out of line" or even "betraying" masculinity. (Connell 83, 213) She mentions that something similar happens in domestic violence between men and women. For some men, wife-beating is a way to "keep them in line". So this has again to do with male dominance and alleged female disobedience. (Connell 83, 213) As a result, the rape of Cate can be seen as the final stage of escalation between both of them, which was built up through multiple attempts of sexualized and abusive violence perpetrated by Ian. It can be assumed that Ian raped Cate because he has the sense of "owning" her. It can be suggested, that he raped her in such a brutish way, because he wanted to punish her for being so disobedient and inflicting "pain" on him by refusing his sexual advances.

In the end, he does not seem to feel any remorse, even though Cate exposes her hate against him throughout the scene. (Kane 2.25, 2.26, 2.27, 2.31, 2.33) Although it is rather unclear why Cate strokes, massages and finally performs oral sex on Ian in this scene, it has to be mentioned that she eventually "[...] bites his penis as hard as she can" (Kane 2.31) leaving him in great pain. (Kane 2.28-2.31) It may be suggested that she did this in revenge for being raped by him the night before. She also rips the sleeves of his jacket off and, as already mentioned, points the gun at him, threatening to shoot his groin. Considering the work by Connell, Ian may be seen as the representation of hegemonic masculinity, whereas Cate may be seen as the representation of feminism, since Connell states in his book, that feminism constantly makes a stand against patriarchy and hegemonic masculinity. (Connell 74)

3.2 The Soldier and Ian

Towards the end of the second scene, we have the appearance of a third character, the soldier. Beforehand, Cate went to the bathroom and we learn that she left the hotel room through the window. (Kane 2.38) Hence we have two male characters left. Actually, the soldier can be seen in two different ways, which I will explain in this chapter.

As the soldier enters the hotel room, the blast did not happen yet, thus the hotel room, Ian's ideal world and his power are still intact. But now, it is threatened by another man and the soldier turns out to be indeed a rival in masculinity. That becomes clear when Ian, wielding his gun, opens the door, after hearing some suspicious knocks and immediately gets disarmed by the soldier. (Kane 2.36) The soldier is furthermore described as carrying a sniper's rifle. (Kane 2.36) Considering what Connell said about guns and masculinity, the soldier not only took Ian's power and masculinity by disarming him, but has from the start the larger signifier of power and masculinity so to speak, the bigger gun.

Being confronted by a much stronger and more dominant male, Ian turns out to be completely helpless and hence becomes very obedient. Being overwhelmed by the soldiers dominance, he not only gives him the rasher of bacon, he was still holding in his hand but the rest of his and Cate's breakfast he had ordered before, as well with only

13

very little resistance. (Kane 2.36-2.37) In this scene, the soldier may be seen as a more dominant male, perhaps a top member of what Connell calls 'hegemonic masculinity', whereas Ian is depicted as a male who is lower in position within the hierarchy of maleness. Compared to the normative approach, which was described earlier in this paper, Ian clearly does not live up to the depiction of masculinity, because in contrast to the soldier, he immediately becomes obedient and does not show the intention to stand his ground.

Subsequently, the soldier not only claims Ian's food, but also his partner. The soldier states that he "[...] can smell the sex" (Kane 2.37) and starts searching the room, finally breaking into the bathroom, revealing that Cate has fled the hotel room. (Kane 2.38) This shows, that the soldier claimed the right to have sex with Cate, since he has the notion of being the more dominant male in this triangle. This is exactly what Ian did when he told Cate that she is more his than Shaun's because he already had sex with her and thus holds the opinion of having the right to claim her. Ian compared the fact that he already has had sex with Cate to being the more dominant male, so to speak. The soldier's argument for being the more dominant male is the fact that he owns the bigger gun. Both of them do not care, that Cate is the partner of somebody else, because they have the notion of having the right to claim her more than the respective rival. When the soldier is looking for Cate, Ian does not dare to attack him in order to defend his "property" but just watches very frightened, which implies that he accepted the soldier's dominance unwillingly. (Kane 2.38) This also can be compared to hegemonic masculinity's successful "claim to authority" (Connell 77), without the need of violence. Ian, depicted as a rather oppressed male, is overwhelmed by this claim and does not dare to stand up against it.

Also, the soldier shows animal-like behaviour when he "[...] very quickly devours both breakfasts" (Kane 2.37) and urinates on Ian's and Cate's pillows, challenging Ian's dominance as some kind of "chief male" in his territory, the hotel room. (Kane 2.39) In the end of the second scene, the hotel room is struck by a mortar bomb, followed by a blackout. (Kane 2.39)

In the beginning of the third scene, the hotel room is completely destroyed due to being struck by a mortar bomb, revealing that the city in fact is a war zone. The blast marks the destruction of Ian's ideal world, his power over Cate and his masculinity. Actually, Kane stated that she pretty much liked the idea of adding a blast in her play that initiates the complete demolition of somebody's life. (Saunders 41)

In this scene, the soldier may represent something else than a top member of 'hegemonic masculinity'. Both laying next to each other, not able to walk as a result of the mortar bomb's impact, they start talking. (Kane 3.39) The soldier tells him gruesome stories about war crimes he committed and about the murder of his girlfriend, Col. That implies, that the soldier is heterosexual. But the stories about him raping men and women alike may be seen as irritating. Also, when the soldier finds a pair of Cate's knickers he asks if they are hers or Ian's, but does not wait for an answer and instead rubs them into his face and smells them with pleasure. (Kane 2.37) I doubt that Kane's intention simply was display that the soldier might be bi-sexual. I rather suggest, it is supposed to indicate that in a context, which is known for its loss of civilized behaviour, like war, social and gender conventions, that were put up by patriarchy and defended by hegemonic masculinity are gone, as well. The soldier does not seem to be interested in somebody's or even his own gender any more. I think the unspeakable brutality that is presented in the play and which was the reason for attacking it may be seen as a method of visualizing that civilization, as we in the western world know it, and all of its rules and conventions stopped existing in the play.

As the soldier asks Ian if he never fucked a man before, or even after he killed him, Ian responds that he of course did not because he is not "queer" (Kane 3.47), which matches the ideals of hegemonic masculinity. Thereby, Ian makes clear that, living up to his principles of manhood, for him it would be completely unmanly to penetrate a man. In contrast to that, the soldier claims that for him it is commonplace to rape men. By doing so, it becomes clear that for him either gender roles and the gendered society does not exist any more or that he carries hegemonic masculinity to the extremes by completely destroying defeated and hence inferior men's masculinities. He mentions that he is "dying to make love [...]" (Kane 3.42) and eventually forces Ian to turn over. (Kane 3.49) He then rapes Ian and pushes his own gun into Ian's anus. (Kane 3.49) Completely helpless, Ian does not defend himself either because he accepted his status as a subordinate man or because he is afraid of being killed. However, after that, the soldier says to Ian: "[...] Can't get tragic about your arse. Don't think your Welsh arse is different to any other arse I fucked." (Kane 3.50) That indicates that it does not matter to him if he has sex with a man or a woman or of which descent the person is, because for him the only thing that counts is that his sexual desire is pleased. It seems like since the war destroyed society, for the soldier, there is neither homosexuality, nor heterosexuality any more.

In contrast to that, due to being raped, Ian sees his masculinity completely fading away. He, who used to be the dominant man and a representative of hegemonic masculinity is put to the end of the hierarchy by a man who either does not care for the patriarchal construction of gender any more, or is the new top representative of hegemonic masculinity in the play. However, hereby he experiences how it feels to be oppressed like he did to women, like Cate, but to other men, like homosexuals and coloured men, as well.

4. Conclusion

All in all, it can be said that clear references to the concept of hegemonic masculinity can be found in Sarah Kane's *Blasted*. Considering the research questions that were asked in the beginning of this term paper, I conclude the results as follows: We learned from Raewyn Connell the concept of hegemonic masculinity actually can be seen as "strategy" serving the purpose of defending the patriarchy and thereby maintaining male dominance and female subordination. Furthermore, we have learned that there even is a gender hierarchy amongst masculinity and that hegemonic masculinity does not only oppress femininity, but other forms of masculinity, that are seen as threat for patriarchy, as well.

Regarding Sarah Kane's play *Blasted*, we can say that the male character Ian may be seen as representative of the hegemonic masculinity in the first two scenes. That can be traced back to Ian not only oppressing the female character Cate, but also by exposing abusive character traits, which result in claiming the right to literally "own" a woman, leading to Ian raping Cate. Not only his sexist view on women, but also his hate of migrants and homosexuals displays his omnipresent urge to oppress people of other gender, race or sexual orientation, which indicates that Ian indeed represents hegemonic masculinity. In this context, we also considered the idea of guns as instruments of gaining and maintaining power and therefore compared them to men's genitalia as symbols of authority and masculinity.

In contrast to that, the soldier may be understood in two different ways. On the one hand, it may be speculated that for the soldier, since war took over, there are no gender relations, no differences between the sexes, no gender conventions any more. Thus, he rapes Ian, who realizes that his ideal world was nothing more but a construct. On the other hand, the soldier may be seen as the complete opposite, as the male of higher rank so to speak, since he owns "the bigger gun" and disarms Ian, thus taking his source of power away from him. Also, the soldier displays a successful, natural claim of power, which Ian immediately capitulates to. Subsequently, the soldier completely oppresses and exploits Ian, like the hegemonic masculinity uses to do with women and inferior men.

Either way, by annihilating Ian's masculinity the soldier allows him to reconsider his position in society. Through Cate growing stronger simultaneously, the gender relations within the play are completely reversed, resulting in Cate becoming the dominant character and Ian being the dependent and helpless character. After all, Cate has mercy with Ian and displays true strength by not exploiting her new position within the restructured gender relation.

Regarding further research, I would recommend to examine the gender relations in further plays by Sarah Kane, since the characters in *Blasted* were perfect examples for analysing masculinity. Moreover, it would be interesting to investigate if there is any connection between Sarah Kane's biography and the depiction of masculinity, in other words if there were specific incidents that influenced her view of men.

Works cited

Primary Sources

Kane, Sarah. *Blasted.* Methuen Publishing Ltd, 2001.

Secondary Sources

Benedict, David. "Disgusting violence? Actually it's quite a peaceful play." *The Independent.* Independent Digital News & Media Ltd, 22 Jan. 1995. Web. 13 May 2020. https://www.independent.co.uk/news/uk/home-news/disgusting-violence-actually-its-quite-a-peaceful-play-1569097.html.

Connell, R. W. *Masculinities.* Cambridge: Polity Press, 2005. Print.

Connell, R. W. and James W. Messerschmidt. "Hegemonic Masculinity. Rethinking the Concept" *Gender & Society* 19.6 (2005): 829-859. Print.

Demetriou, Demetrakis Z. "Connell's concept of hegemonic masculinity: A critique." *Theory and Society* 30.3 (2001): 337-361. Print.

Iball, Helen. *Sarah Kane's Blasted.* London: Continuum International Publishing Group, 2008. Print.

Saunders, Graham. 'Love me or kill me' Sarah Kane and the theatre of extremes. Manchester: Manchester University Press, 2016. Print.